ZEN and ALWAYS

El Morya's Treasury of Spiritual Quips

David Christopher Lewis

MERU PRESS

NOW, ZEN AND ALWAYS

El Morya's Treasury of Spiritual Quips

David Christopher Lewis

A special thank you to the Nicholas Roerich Museum, New York, NY, for the use of a portion of the Nicholas Roerich painting *Fiat Rex* on the back cover.

Cover design by N. Thomas Miller
Compilation by Debra LeMore and Joyce Genis

ISBN 978-0-9818863-0-5
1. Spirituality 2. New Age

Published by MERU PRESS®
Printed in the United States of America

Additional copies, write to
THE HEARTS CENTER®
P.O. BOX 277 • LIVINGSTON, MONTANA 59047

For more information:
(630) 894-4410
www.theheartscenter.org
friends@theheartscenter.org

This book is dedicated
to beloved El Morya
whose eternal spirit of joy
guides us daily in fulfilling
the Will of God.

Perfume the air
with the fragrance
of your heart.

El Morya

EL MORYA

artist: Tom Miller

CONTENTS

INTRODUCTION

El Morya. Just musing on the name or letting it resonate in my mind brings about an internal shift and alignment of consciousness, a deepening awareness of God-reality and beingness within. El Morya—co-founder of Theosophy with Kuthumi. El Morya—Eastern adept from whom many insightful wisdom teachings flowed to his Russian amanuenses—Nicholas and Helena Roerich. El Morya—of whom one especially devoted disciple once penned, "I loved him before I knew him."

El Morya—Chohan of the Will of God for mankind, progenitor of numberless generations as the archetypal father-figure Abraham, noble knight of the famed Round Table era as King Arthur, staunch ally of God as the learned and illustrious Thomas More, Mogul emperor Akbar who conquered many Asiatic lands and peoples but whose visionary leadership and compassionate acceptance of all religious persuasions is historic and could be universally applied to mankind's great benefit today.

When El Morya came to me to begin dictating these charming nuggets of wisdom, which he termed "quips," I was somewhat in awe, having read many of the often enigmatic but power-packed verses in his Agni Yoga releases. As I received them, my heart leapt. I often laughed within, witnessing his cosmic humor unfold as I penned each line. My inner vision increased during these sessions when his radiance, his noble view on life were transferred to my mind.

El Morya is a no-nonsense master. He can concentrate into a few words the essence of the Godhead that can change us forever. As his heart-mind connection is melded with ours, we can't help but rise in consciousness to see life from a newer, more objective and more loving and forgiving perspective—a godly, bird's eye view.

In this book we have included El Morya's Quips as they were originally and chronologically released from September to December of 2005. There may seem to be repetitions, but the master often re-emphasizes the core teachings of truth because we tend to forget them in our daily lives, interactions and relationships. We may try reading them in the greater context of the master's purpose—to help us evolve beyond our current, limited mind-sets with his Zen wisdom.

Too sparse in today's superficial communication is the empowered and artful delivery of divine inspiration. Knowing that in our own busy lives we often take time to catch only media sound bites of information here and there, El Morya uses this means to deliver concise morsels of truth. "Master for All Seasons," he comes to win us over to his true-blue frequencies of higher gnosis. Resting in his presence of joy, we contemplate our own solar awareness that will help reconnect us with our Source.

As you chuckle and muse with the master upon reading his quips, El Morya says, "O humble traveler on the road of life, become the adept, become the master."

David Christopher Lewis
Paradise Valley, Montana

WHO ARE THE ASCENDED MASTERS?

The ascended masters are our elder brothers and sisters who have passed all major initiations of the spiritual path and graduated from Earth's schoolroom—by free will returning to the heart of God through the sacred ritual or process known as the ascension. They are the "saints robed in white" of East and West—of all religions and cultures—who stand in glory before the Presence of the one God.

The ascension is complete liberation from the rounds of karma and rebirth or reincarnation whereby the soul is merged with its Divine Presence, also known as the Higher Self or Solar Source. It is spiritual enlightenment and freedom from the gravitational or karmic pull of the Earth. It is the bliss of beingness within God's holy light and eternal Presence of pure, divine love.

The ascended masters are our teachers

and guides, showing us the way Home through a pathway that is unique for each person and yet requires a determined self-discipline and balance in our daily lives. Meditation and silent contemplation, as well as the giving of prayers, mantras, decrees and songs, can help us in this process. Balancing our past negative karma through service to those whom we have wronged is also a major key to our victory. The ascended masters exemplify the highest qualities of the Godhead through their givingness to all life, having mastered the initiations of the seven rainbow rays or flames throughout many lifetimes of service to life.

Examples of ascended masters whom many may recognize are Jesus, Mother Mary, Saint Joseph (Saint Germain), Saint Francis (Kuthumi), El Morya, Padre Pio, Gautama Buddha, Lord Maitreya, Padma Sambhava, Kuan Yin, Krishna, Confucius, Lao Tse, Zarathustra, Enoch and Melchizedek. However, there are also many unsung heroes and heroines of the Spirit who have transcended our earthly domain in recent decades who also serve from the ascended level.

The Masters of Wisdom teach us that we, too, may ascend at the close of this lifetime if we fully utilize our gifts and talents and balance at least fifty-one percent of our karma while also fulfilling our personal mission through service to life while balancing the flames of love, wisdom and power within our hearts. The goal of life is oneness with our Source through the ascension and the ascended masters most beautifully lead the way for us all.

WHAT IS A DICTATION?

A dictation is a message delivered by an ascended master, angel or cosmic being to an anointed and sponsored messenger through the agency of the Holy Spirit by special dispensation. A dictation may be delivered in numerous ways, although the most common is through telepathic communication between the master and the messenger. The messages may be written, typed or delivered orally. In the case of *ex cathedra* dictations, the master's presence is so tangible over the messenger that the oral delivery is as if the master is physically speaking through the messenger's vocal chords.

During a dictation, the master's spiritual light energy or radiation is tangibly felt by the messenger who becomes a conduit for the transmission of both the message and the divine radiance of the master's presence or higher consciousness. The radiation is often so great that all who listen or who are in close proximity to the dictation can feel a tremendous rush of spiritual light and energy during its transmission, even if it is heard via recording after the fact.

A dictation of an ascended master is not psychic channeling through a medium wherein messages may come from disembodied spirits who are not ascended in the light and free. By cosmic law, sponsored and anointed messengers may only receive dictations from God-free beings and not those who dwell in the astral or psychic (emotional) plane of the Earth.

Each dictation is a spiritual experience and opportunity for the devotee to be an active participant in the delivery of the dictation through conscious awareness of the sacred process that occurs during the preparation for the master's coming as well as the actual message itself. During the time of preparation there is a heightened sense of spiritual light in the room where the delivery occurs.

The messenger prepares his or her consciousness for the master's delivery through silent or deep meditation and concentration upon the light of God within the master's holy presence. And there is a heightened sensitivity to all vibrations in the surrounding area that may affect the transmission itself. Thus, for oral dictations, it is imperative that those in the audience remain centered, silent and in a state of deep reverence and devotion while listening. Each participant may thus help to "anchor" the message and the radiation behind the message during the dictation itself.

Another term for a dictation is a HeartStream, for truly each dictation is delivered with great love. And the spiritual light within it is accentuated and flows through the heart chakra of the messenger to bless all who receive it. For those whose inner sight is opened, they may see the master's presence over the messenger with great streams of light pouring forth into the room and unto the Earth through the chakras of the master overshadowing those of the messenger.

Every dictation contains spiritual keys for all who hear or read it for their progress on the path toward their ultimate freedom and ascension in the light. Thus every dictation is a blessing and an opportunity for the devotee to rise higher in consciousness through the wisdom teaching of the master.

WHAT IS HEARTSTREAMING?

by El Morya

Heartstreaming is the emanation of divine love from and through one's heart center, the central of the seven major chakras of the spiritual or etheric body of sons and daughters of God. It is the science of connecting with one's Higher Self or Divine Presence by attuning to the frequencies of the Spirit through deep meditation, prayer and devotion. It is contacting one's Solar Presence or Source and allowing a sacred flow of radiant light-energy to consciously course through one's being to bring joy, love, harmony and peace to the world.

Heartstreaming is an ancient art and yet one that all can know today by learning the science of Presence or living in the Eternal Now. While heartstreaming, one feels an increase in the vitality of light and life within as an inner joy, leaving off of living on the periphery of life and entering the heights of cosmic gnosis or inner wisdom born of truth in the sublime and higher worlds of existence. By attending to one's heart connection with the Eternal One, a constant stream of contact may be maintained and a higher understanding of one's purpose and mission in life found.

Heartstreaming occurs when one pours devotion, praise and thanksgiving to God through prayer, mantra, chant and song. It occurs when one is engaged in reverential contemplation upon divine principles, values and precepts so long as it is born of love and mindfulness and not just a mental exercise.

Heartstreaming with others in a group setting allows for a greater interactivity of all the divine resources of light within that group when each one is focused on holy purpose, visualizing the beautiful outcome that the group would see as manifest in its spiritual work. There is a multiplication factor of the divine energy that flows through the group by the square of the number of those present. And thus great spiritual power, wisdom and love may be wielded, augmented by ascended beings when heartstreaming occurs through the heart-centeredness of each one present through the harmonious alchemy of the many.

Heartstreaming with ascended masters occurs when the deity is called upon in their names as divine intermediaries—the saints and sages of East and West—who have gained their enlightenment and liberation from the rounds of karma and rebirth by oneness with God. During this time of sacred interaction, a master may communicate through an anointed representative who is trained in the science of being as an amanuensis through the spiritual disciplines of the path but most especially through humility and love. Through discourse, darshan and dictation, the light body of the master is fully present and radiates spiritual energies through the chakras of the messenger of light unto all present, and to all who are participating through their conscious awareness in viewing or listening to the message of the master.

You may also rise in consciousness into the higher realms of light to directly heartstream with any ascended master, angel, cosmic being, or your personal sponsoring master, as you gain adeptship and attainment through maintaining your divine connection by practicing holy Presence day and night. Thus, heartstreaming is a sacred event each time it occurs in whatever way you, the disciple, set forth by intention your purpose in that moment.

There is a great stream of light that is coursing through the Earth body itself in many planes of being that you may enter in consciousness through the sensitivity of your spiritual faculties. And when you enter the great heartstream of God as it courses through life itself, you may truly understand what it means to live in the very heart of God.

Every Christ, every Buddha, and all who have gained oneness with the divine, are here to assist you in mastering the science and art of heartstreaming. You attend to, through communication with your Higher Source, the requirements of your soul day by day as you strive to pass your initiations on the Path.

And thus, each and every ascended master is happy and feels privileged when called upon by name, or simply by recognition, to heartstream with you toward the holy purpose of your personal enlightenment and freedom, blessed ones.

I am the Master M and my heartstream is available to you this day and every day, this moment and every moment for your victory!

I thank you.

EL MORYA WILL GUIDE

El Morya will guide.
El Morya will lead.
The blue-ray focus of M's mighty steed
flashes 'cross the mind,
Thunders to victory, action.
Onward to M's sign of a will
that hath no faction.

Ho! It is M of the Himavat.*
Ho! The blue-ray master!
M, it is M of the Himavat,
marching, marching faster.

Action, movement, victory.
Action, courage, speed.
Action, joy, nobility.
Action, labor, achieve!

Lighthouse, bridge, port, ship,
arrow, ray, beacon, tower.
Lapis, diamonds, crystal, mist,
leaves, garden, flowers.

Infinite archer's flight.
A quest for the right.
M's abode in sight.
A citadel of light.

M, it is M of the Himavat.
Ho! He calls from his mountain.
Come up hither, OM TAT SAT,
beckoning us to his fountain.

*Himavat (himavant) is the Hindu God of snow, a personification of the Himalayan mountains.

Written by Brian Sweeney. Used by permission.

EL MORYA'S TREASURY OF SPIRITUAL QUIPS

Part One

August 27, 2005

1. Be flexible.
2. Respect your elders.
3. Breathe deeply.
4. Enjoy the sun and the light.
5. Know transcendence.
6. Arrange your time so as to commend the brethren.
7. Be fruitful.
8. Fine tune your senses and listen to the music of life.
9. Position your heart to hear the cries of those in need.

10. Train your vision on perfect symmetry, for it awakens the God intent within.
11. Fan the flame of purity through stillness.
12. Be, in spite of all who would have you not be.
13. Pulse out light in waves of cosmic understanding.
14. Release the past and the future and stay in the now.
15. Grow into the unshadowed radiance of your Higher Self.
16. Quicken your desire to serve, for in serving you will lose your self.
17. Find the treasure within others and you will never know want.
18. Reveal who you are to yourself a little more each day.
19. Intend to find the secret of the treasure trove within, and all shall be brought forth in time to satisfy every Godly desire.

20. Discern the varieties of paths and help others take the first step.

21. Be my man, my woman of courage who knows that victory is a flame that must be lit and sustained.

22. Qualify your thoughts with the radiance of Love.

23. Refinish your basement often, for in the foundation are found the true resources of the spiritual life.

24. Blend your voice with every angel, for they love to sing of light to the Father-Mother of Lights.

25. Love with a gentle smile of grace and in your eyes others will discover themSelves.

26. Complete only the next step and then a new and higher one will appear before you.

27. Gain a new deva friend daily and you will never be lonely.

28. Allocate the proper resources to study your emotions and the flow of energy within the wires of your electronic body and you will discover the true station of its source.

29. Be kind, for when you are all will know you.

30. Blend your mind into the stream of infinite grace.

31. Pattern your days after the movement of the sun and your nights upon that of the stars, and the eternal dream of God will lead you.

32. Be joyous in the new discovery of fortitude in the breath of the newborn.

August 28, 2005

33. Release your hold on the past and experience life.

34. Galvanize your speech with the dynamo of right thought.

35. Why not know who you are now?
36. Rhythm in the midst of chaos is my song.
37. The space between you and You must be closed.
38. Create new space for God in the laboratory of your heart.
39. Invest in the infinite possibilities of love.
40. Growth results from opportunity taken to reach for the sun.
41. Consume the pride of unknowing, for it is always ignorant.
42. Ventilate your mind with new wisdom.
43. Impeccable must be your desirelessness.
44. Plan to be God and then make it happen.
45. Release grand ideas into the fertile soil of your soul.
46. Commend your vision to the belief in the unlimited One.

47. Organize your world around the first ray of the dawn.

48. Increase the potency of your God ideas to elicit change.

49. Concur with your Self before deciding how to thrust forward.

50. Each trial allows the Great Arbitrator to direct your course.

51. Why ask others when the answer lies within?

52. The point of the nexus can become the point of critical mass if you will to make it so.

53. Puny hearts cannot grasp grand possibilities.

54. To be or not, that is the question at the "Y" which is now.

55. The realms of glory are hidden only by your own shades.

56. Trust in the grand scheme of the divine playwright, for he knows the final act.

57. Rewrite history today through forgiveness.
58. Inculcate in the next generation the need to transcend yours.
59. Blend your mind into the stream of infinite grace.
60. Rescind your past decisions to sleep on.
61. Keep the tempo even when the Great Maestro's hands become a blur.
62. Call forth the fire of Prometheus into the domain of your heart.
63. Tutor your soul in the art of compassionate communication.
64. Blame not others for options you have accepted.
65. The final ascent, though intense, is full of prana.

August 29, 2005

66. Practice the art of divine love through

the giving of yourself in totality.

67. The intensity of your path is determined by the radiance of your heart brought to bear in all you think, do and say.

68. The qualities of love that you bestow determine the richness of your spiritual life.

69. As important as your relationship with others is your relationship with your Self.

70. Perfection is the goal; pure love is the means; wisdom is the wayshower.

71. Ideals cannot be won through brute force. Compassion magnetizes them unto us.

72. Revelation comes when we least expect it but when we most need it.

73. The joy of the path is ascension's catalyst.

74. Being is both a science and an art.

75. Although justice is blind, she hears every cry for mercy.

76. The gift of life must be cherished.

77. Those who murder the unborn will never know eternal life.

78. Grace is earned by compassion, kindness and mercy.

79. If you seek to buy love, the price will always be beyond your income.

80. Glory in the light of purity and your halo shall glow.

81. Everyone needs an exit strategy from self-delusion.

82. The path is strewn with the bones of those who could not surrender and with the crutches of those who have.

83. Practice the art of giving and you will learn the alchemy of abundance.

84. Begin each assignment with the outbreath of gratitude and the inbreath of cosmic expectancy.

85. The only omen you need is that of your Presence.

86. Reveal the inner light in others and you will be tanned by their rays.

87. Conclude every day with praise for the layers of unreality that were revealed and more importantly those that were shed.

88. Intertwine your desires with surrender and your hopes with giving and all will be fulfilled.

89. Recreate yourself daily and you will outlast death.

90. The only sin is failure to act when you have been given the map to your own divinity.

91. Those who think God ceased to create after the sixth day have never discerned the meaning of recreation.

92. More important than exercising your brain is jumpstarting your heart.

93. Forget brainstorming; begin heartstreaming!

94. Reduce your caloric intake of fear and munch instead on pure joy.
95. Learn to exercise your mind through the breathstrokes of your heart and lungs.
96. Don't let the bliss of ignorance and the mists of maya become the abyss of death.
97. Awaken to the sun of wisdom.

August 30, 2005

98. Realize that all is not well when your mind is too busy to rest in peace.
99. Portents are sent to you to provide a way out of ignorance.
100. Cover your head only from the illogic of mindlessness.
101. Attune the strings of your heart to the Maestro's ear.
102. Compel yourself to annihilate all voices of animal reasoning.

103. When you increase the velocity of your love, the axles of depression will stop.

104. The seasons to be Godly are summer, winter, spring and fall.

105. Increase the volume of the inner voice.

106. Attunement is not a matter of grandiosity but of stillness.

107. Recreation should be your daily vitamin.

108. Seniority is only valid when measuring spiritual attainment.

109. Rainbows should remind us of the hard work it takes to weather the storms of doom.

110. Bringing a smile to a child in need brings eons of hope to the angels.

111. Replenishing your charity should be as easy as filling the salt shaker.

112. Tantalize the world by the gift of divine laughter you elicit because you care.

113. Transcending time and space can be as quick as boiling water if you supply the fire.

114. To reveal the hour of victory beforehand is tantamount to drugging your own child.

115. Come to grips with the fact that you will always be a work in progress.

116. Those who think that they have attained should observe a dozen newborn babies for a month.

117. Parallel to your own path is one that you best not take but should not ignore.

118. Intend to create a world of beauty and the divine artisan will provide the oils.

119. Polish your aura in the refiner's fire of striving.

120. Complete each assignment without thought of the grade.

121. Fill every ounce of opportunity with nothing but gratitude and your scales shall balance.

122. Remind yourself to have fun, especially when silliness could lead to your retirement.

123. Don't wash your aura in others' swill.

124. Carve out a niche for God to get through to your heart.

125. Paint your days with fresh colors and be happy.

126. Poverty will not be vanquished until greed is uprooted, especially in the poor.

September 5, 2005

127. I seek accomplices.

128. Graciously receive all who come to the door.

129. To this end work: the end of life as you, the beginning of life as God.

130. Tend the flock with gentility.

131. We see who you are, not who you aren't.

132. Involve yourself in God's affairs.

133. Why seek human advice when your divine course is set before you?

134. I Am a Workman of the Lord.

135. Invite your cells to the divine laboratory, then inculcate in them the need to change.

136. Complete every endeavor with a silent prayer.

137. Involve yourself only in matters of the heart.

138. The Lord of the vineyard planted it long before he hired you.

139. Incumbent upon incumbents: Do the will of the ones who sent you.

140. Today's commercials are full of ad-vice.

141. Potential is just that. Everyone has it. Few use it.

142. Create in your mind's eye God's.

143. Trust in your ability to become and you shall.

144. Plenty of work awaits those who know me.

145. Invisible partners are always ready to assist you. Use them.

146. Position yourself always to hear the voice of God. Having heard, obey.

147. Ignore the cacophony of voices that ignore the one that is true.

148. Plumage is only important when it is made of fire.

149. Look inward.

150. Correct your thinking.

151. Ingest more light food.

152. Groundbreaking changes come to those who slay the personal undertaker.

153. For a spiritual transfusion look to the unlimited supply in God's heart.

154. Change your polarity through the positive ion of the Divine Atom.

155. Into the domain of your heart I stream my momentum of will-love.

156. Cause the effect you seek now.

157. Trade in your junker for a new model.

158. Sleep is the disease of all mankind.

159. Plot good.

September 8, 2005 I

160. Radiate light through an infectious smile and a serene heart.

161. Become as pure as water and you will discern the secrets of creation.

162. Know the sun, not only its rays.

163. Impress upon life the image of yourself that God invested you with before your first breath.

164. To love is to surrender.

165. To give is to offer only what you have become, for then you can become more.

166. Realization of your divinity doesn't happen in a day, it happens moment by moment.

167. Truth is not only stranger than fiction, it is a certain synthesis of fact and fiction.

168. Investing only in material goods will bring only material happiness. Investing in divine goods will bring eternal joy.

169. Complete your reason for being by Being.

170. To know your Self, surrender the self in the mirror of God's great reflecting pool.

171. Perfume the air with the fragrance of your heart.

172. Intend to love always and you shall.

173. If your world and life are governed by grace, then your heart will sing.

174. Travel lightly, for this allows you to light everywhere you travel.

175. Compel others only through your example.

176. To bless others you must first receive light from the Originator of blessings.

177. A compendium of wisdom must not be left on the dusty shelves but read and put into play daily.

178. Awaken each day in total awe of the beauty of life and begin your journey anew.

179. Those who do not study history cannot be entrusted with the future.

180. Cosmic consciousness may only come when your view is expanded beyond the domain of your own world.

181. To surrender is to begin to know love.

182. Travel nightly to the stars and a new geography, a new history and a new cosmology will be yours.

183. Become historians of light in the affairs of mankind.

184. Are you ready for the next step? Then proceed with beauty and a guarded abandon!

185. If your only intent is to reach for and eat the apple, you will never experience the joy of climbing the tree.

186. Great thinkers invest in solitude, for only in the soundless silence may the divine voice be heard.

187. Fire must be studied, comprehended, internalized and lastly delivered.

September 8, 2005 II

188. Into the domain of the heart must every spirit seek solace, for only in its fires will be known its native estate.

189. Your world is what you make it by every thought, word and deed.

190. In judging others you lose a portion of the energy you need to make it on the path.

191. The stream of pure consciousness must not be clouded by others' misguided contributions.

192. Continue to press on, even when others attempt to iron your wrinkles.

193. Blame not your Self for your own shortcomings.

194. Police will not be needed when the civility of divine ethics is inculcated in all, beginning even before conception.

195. True grit agitates only those whose edges have not been worn away with the searing sands of experience.

196. Complete one task daily—love.

197. Time and space are only real to those who live in their grip.

198. Prepare to receive every need and then move on. All will be supplied in due course because you have forgotten your needs and only serve to meet those of others.

199. Blessings come to those who pass them on without hesitation.

200. Realize the joy of intense identification with the divine One.

201. If you would see, purify your vision of others.

202. Increase your power through humility and surrender.

203. Become a lightbearer, but make sure your torch does not scorch those whose wicks are not ready to be lit.

204. Enjoy being a son or a daughter of God. It is your birthright to be happy.

205. Intensify your state of relaxation as you prepare to climb the steep hills of life.

206. Include in your prospectus to the

divine employer the gift of loving obedience.

207. Conclude each victory with a bow of gratitude and a new vow of surrender.

208. Present not your best effort but your brightest service and greatest selflessness.

209. Only in the eyes of God will you see the true nature of goodness in everyone.

210. Cycles of wellness are intermixed with periods of illness in order to bring wholeness.

211. If you love everyone equally, be prepared to receive the envy and vilification of those who expect something more than you can, by cosmic law, give.

212. Pray without ceasing, and invite the prayer to resonate while your voice is in the repose of caressing the divine One in complete silence.

213. Experiencing bliss is not the means but the result of your spiritual practice.

214. Spiritual freedom comes to those who have won it through a sacrificial life.

215. Becoming a true messenger is tantamount to becoming the instrument of the divine ventriloquist.

September 8, 2005 III

216. Take a recess from your ego and a sabbatical from your dweller. Then you'll know peace.

217. Inherent within every answer that we deliver is a challenge to come up higher.

218. It is imperative that everyone has quality time with one's GodParents.

219. Treason is the treachery that leads a soul to the betrayal of its reason for being. In short, it is the treachery of human reasoning.

220. Into space cast your highest hopes and one day your line will bring their reward.

221. Some have told you to seize the day; I tell you to lay siege to the moment!

222. All great *bodhisattvas* walk in the moccasins of mercy.

223. Perfection should not be a goal but a present reality accepted.

224. If we could see all, we would beg the divine optometrist for rose-colored glasses.

225. Input your prayers into the great database of God's computer.

226. Though everyone has foibles, few have the gall to admit it.

227. If you think you have all your marbles then try to fly.

228. Being true to yourself means surrendering every skeleton in your closet.

229. The best composite you can create contains a mixture of you and God, and the best colloid is you suspended in the ocean of God.

230. Facts are only excuses for those who require proof. The divine equation is foolproof.

231. Pretend that you can and in childlike simplicity you will.

232. If you think you've done it all, you haven't met the fat lady. If you have, give her the score anyway.

233. Glory in the rays of the dawn but don't be lax in applying the oil of work.

234. Create a new sense of the urgency to follow your Self into eternity now.

235. Give up the idea that you can't and thereby embrace the mind of God.

236. It is imperative that every devotee learn to adore the God within.

237. If you could see what we see, you

would know why we chose the higher way.

238. Once you attain to the fullness of who you are, you will meet your long-lost friends.

239. Seek as friends only those who will hold up your mirror in your darkest hour—and who will also switch on the light.

240. We have long ago dispensed with the word "incredible."

241. Those who are full of themselves can never become *arhats*.

242. Believe in the Great Magician and he will never perform a disappearing act.

September 9, 2005 I

243. Releasing yourself from guilt, move forward into acceptance of your divinity now.

244. Build a field of belief around yourself by planting seeds of love everywhere.

245. When the Creator intends to blend his music with yours don't insist on being a soloist.

246. Inherent in every test of personal initiative to overcome some ancient karma is the exact quotient of energy needed to be victorious.

247. Revelation may only occur when you have pulled the wool back from your own eyes.

248. My message is complex yet simple: Get the point and you will have the key to the apex of the entire cone of its manifestation.

249. With all your understanding, stand firmly under the present reality of God's availability to be where you are.

250. Magic is not so mysterious to those who have seen its hand.

251. Reverse the polarity of downward spirals if you seek to rise.

252. If you would be loved, then be love.

253. Incumbent upon the adept is the necessity to accept at every moment, without pride, the fullness of one's attainment.

254. Congruency is the key to your divine reality.

255. Those who cannot rise above their animal nature will remain in the doghouse of mediocrity.

256. Create a new sense of the ownership of the Creator's Will within you, for change is the first requisite for its deed.

257. Don't erase the tracings of your reality that the divine architect drew on the blueprint of your spirit.

258. Accept the inevitable: you are divine.

259. Watch your words. See their effects. Then speak your truth.

260. A messenger's job is to deliver his master's words exactly as they were conveyed. This requires a deep trust between the two as well as the ability of the messenger to master the art of

listening and speaking simultaneously. It is not so mysterious.

September 9, 2005 II

261. My diamond heart is sufficient to stabilize thine.

262. Create the thoughtform that the Earth has become a star and then work to make it happen.

263. Your success is dependent upon your focus.

264. Twin flames are not only four times more powerful than a single flame, they create multidimensionally and may fuse spirit and matter.

265. Realization is the ionization of the real within you.

266. To travel in spirit, seek first a divine travel agent.

267. Externalize the internal fire. Internalize the external fire. Breathe light.

268. Becoming attuned is no longer a concern for those who maintain the dial on the proper channel at all times.

269. Becoming a pure vessel is easy. Setting sail without wind is the test.

270. Study trees and then emulate them.

271. Provide to all the key not to Self-transcendence but to Self-declaration.

272. Purification must always precede divination.

273. Collect your thoughts, but then let them fly!

274. Enjoy living in the sphere in which you abide, for only when mastered with joy may you move on.

275. Imperative is the need of the adept to attend to the affairs of the Godhead diligently.

276. Cast not your diamonds to the dogs but woo them by a morsel, no more.

277. Use enemies as a platform upon which

to rise to new levels of compassion.

278. Study the eyes of all, for therein you may discern their true nature.

279. Pool your resources not with sharks but with dolphins.

280. Pass on invitations from those who know not the value of your work.

281. Although the greatest teacher is example, the greatest example is love in action.

282. Perfume the world with the essential oil of your kindness.

283. Don't mystify your charge with superfluous words. When less is said the void may be filled with your mutual Presence.

284. Prevent spiritual arteriosclerosis by ingesting only divine food.

285. Potent is the Infinite One's uncanny ability to shake us up just when our salt has become too crystallized.

286. Young pets have a way of bringing out the child within us. Let your children see your true nature.

September 10, 2005

287. From dust thou cameth, to stardust thou goeth.

288. Creative tension keeps the rope taut but the noose in check.

289. Learn the greatest skill—to hear and obey the divine voice, and the greatest trade—to be under its employ always.

290. Reason is to gnosis as pity is to compassion.

291. Step through the mirror of illusion into the world of reality and never look back.

292. Qualify every act with heart and it will be acceptable to divine eyes.

293. Employ your mind as the fine instrument it is, and play diatonic scales never imagined.

294. Release the sense of lack. Everything you need is always available everywhere.

295. To find the pot of gold at the end of the rainbow inspect the treasure chest of your heart.

296. Ceaseless blessings flow to you who pray to save sentient beings, for aren't you one of them?

297. Intention is not action, but it's a good warm-up.

298. If you dream but don't act, your clay will crack.

299. Create a new you daily and you won't be dissatisfied with what you see in the mirror.

300. Get out the maps, ropes and grappling hooks and scale with me a new summit. Together we'll enjoy the air and the view.

301. If you haven't been humbled you've never lived.

302. When learning the art of cooking, don't forget the fire and the oil.

303. Improve your rhythm. Dance to the heartbeat of the invisible Maestro.

304. Mind-stuff should be fashioned into crystal lattices before the great laser of creative intelligence is fired up.

305. Complete every trek with a final breath of surrender.

306. It is imperative that heartfriends relinquish pride before community is formed.

307. The greatest pension plan is a causal body replete with spiritual fruits ripened by the sunshine of your love.

308. Foreign to every community should be those who will not contribute. We desire not a conglomerate of individualists.

309. Trust in the Great Initiator and then pass today's exam.

310. Prove your Self-worth through action.

311. Communities are only as strong as their weakest member, so raise the standard.

312. Glorify not self. Prepare the laurel for the invisible warrior.

313. Provide me with seven and I will save the city and with seventy and I will save the nation.

314. Become adept at being and you shall be an adept.

September 14, 2005

315. You are what you assimilate.

316. Looks can be deceiving. Rely on your Vision.

317. Trust in the Lord builds the surest bridge to divine union.

318. Captivate yourself in the expanse of the Great Mind.

319. Close the door to every vagrant thought.

320. Princes and paupers both have opportunity.

321. Impeach concepts that have lost their savor.

322. Conclude your meditations with a smile.

323. Fill your mind with emptiness.

324. Do you purport to be an adept?
Try again.

325. Ice cream may soothe the palate but what will soothe the soul?

326. Don't go dry. Ask the divine honer to whet you.

327. Compress time into *now*-noseconds.

328. Rely on the bed-rock of divine reason.

329. Prevent yourself and produce unlimited results.

330. Don't vent your feelings. Aerate your spirit.

331. Comply only with the laws of universal life.

332. Ride the tide of God's love.

333. Sandy beaches are not for those who would be spiritually tanned.

334. God created the void first.

335. Closing your mind will only open Pandora's box.

336. Firmness is necessary for mattresses and minds but not hearts.

337. The infirm should not lead you into battle.

338. Conscious living is the first requisite.

339. If you tend to give up, then surrender it once and for all.

340. I invest in those who desire prophet-sharing.

341. Confess who You are.

342. Transcend time and space. Ascend daily.

343. Don't be so quick to react. Jump instead.

344. My most compelling argument is none at all.

345. Intuit.

346. Love cannot be created, only blended.

347. Forever is quite long. Begin here. Start now.

348. Create a stream of laser love. Intensify light through your heart.

349. When you don't know the answer, go back to the solution.

350. It is problematic not to be.

September 15, 2005

351. Choose your trainer well.

352. Keep up with me.

353. I know quality rocks.

354. Depend on God.

355. When you need direction study the wind.

356. Intensify divine reliance.

357. Don't beg forgiveness, emit it.

358. Visualize perfection.

359. Immerse yourself in my diamond reality.

360. Prevail even when the winds do.

361. Travel with me. I am the map and compass.

362. I prefer the intrepid.

363. Ignore simpletons.

364. Pride is the fall.

365. Those who walk with me will fly.

366. Impel action.

367. Pre-face your appearance with compassion.

368. Vend only to those willing to pay all.

369. Don't just study cycles, race on them.

370. Creature comforts are best left to the dogs.

371. My boot camp is the best.

September 16, 2005

372. Once upon a time there was none.

373. Out of the blue, I AM.

374. Resound the soundless song of love.

375. Contribute the all of your nothingness everywhere, always.

376. Create anew the You God knew.

377. Realizing your potential is only the beginning. Accelerate to infinity times your potential.

378. Every problem is a past karmic entanglement to be dissolved by forgiveness and redirected through love.

379. Cursing must be turned into divine nursing.

380. Greater flow requires an open spigot.

381. Turn down your ego.

382. Billowing white clouds become violent tornados through one angry thought.

383. Forgiveness is the great universal solvent.

384. Complex equations often require only one factor to be solved.

385. You are a conundrum to all but your Creator.

386. If you've failed at least there's Hope.

387. Love is not only written in the air, it is punctuated in the stars and versed in the galaxies.

388. Long for desirelessness.

389. Those who see don't need to believe, but it's best if they do.

390. Our work is not about avoiding impending disaster but about creating new stars.

391. Invest in what money can't buy.

392. Bossy generals aren't needed when the troops know the mission.

393. Study fluorescence. Better, investigate laser optics. Best, become a pulsar.

394. Don't let quantity be an excuse for quality. Host and serve both.

395. Redundancy requires adeptship.

396. Clear minds thrive.

397. Euthanasia is not our way. Pain leads the way to enlightenment.

398. Refresh yourself in the river of life.

399. Become a chandelier and then remain dust free.

400. I walk quickly. Follow my steps.

401. Value the power of a helping hand.

402. My X factor is the staying power of Love.

403. Don't follow your heart, lead with it.

404. Your destiny is starhood, not stardom.

September 21, 2005

405. Fend for your Self.

406. The best presents (Presence) you can give is yours.

407. I deliver friendly fire.

408. Fortunately I decided to do the Will of God.

409. I'm a man for all seasons but also one of few words.

410. Quality leadership isn't an oxymoron in heaven.

411. If we depended on mankind we'd prefer to reembody.

412. Serving aces is my great joy.

413. My word is not final, but enough.

414. I seek those who not only see but do the Will of God.

415. Our investiture ceremonies are invisible to the naked I.

416. I love you regardless of what you were, who you are and when you will become.

417. Just do it perfectly.

418. If you stay on top of things you'll never know defeat.

419. Three keys to Buddhahood. Waste not. Want not. Why not.

420. If you forget me you haven't known me.

421. Wrap your Self up in what you do.

422. Conceptualize with me daily your own perfection.

423. If I only intended, I wouldn't be.

424. *Trans*-mutation is the only type we allow.

425. All proceeds should be carefully planted again.

426. Include in your plans a word from The Word.

427. Meditate on a hot iron and build great Self steam.

428. Air your problems with me on your knee and I'll see what can be.

429. Infinite possibilities are just that.

430. The blind by nature block out the sun.

431. Create a new you. Unsubscribe to all but who you are.

432. Wouldn't you rather gather with your Father?

433. Meditate on sunflowers.

434. Too many films will create one on you.

435. Rely on your immaculate conceptions.

436. Quest for the best jest with me.

437. I will never leave those who believe.

September 22, 2005

438. Apathetic parenting produces offensive offspring.

439. Wear your heart not only on your sleeve but everywhere.

440. Don't let God be the sole lover of your soul.

441. Grow your will as a bamboo plant and your love as a redwood.

442. Let each rinse and dry cycle leave less on your karmic tunic.

443. My favorite four-letter words: More love.

444. Like a sun, increase the reach of your warmth.

445. I follow the order of the Divine Mother: steady as she goes.

446. Proving yourself right doesn't mean you should take the left-handed path.

447. When saying to others, "I Am the

Way," make sure you've been to the end of the road and back first.

448. Many who would be king should let their realm be the depths of their heart.

449. The eightfold path is the Buddhic way to infinity.

450. If you're a slave to your emotions your emancipation will elude you.

451. Make *aha* experiences *aha*bit.

452. Prevent prevarication by downloading eternal truths from God's mainframe.

453. Gain your freedom by increasing the expansiveness of your love.

454. I trust in God and thereby I always win.

455. Learn the art of tact, let Theos act within you.

456. Be a diplomat of healing. Divest yourself of the petty and low matters of mankind and make the divine proof of love manifest in truth.

457. If everyone invests a pound of love daily, with compound interest we will change the whole world in a fortnight.

458. My favorite song: More amor.

459. If you don't get dirty you'll never reach the bedrock of love.

460. Collapse the lapses in your love through time-released compassion.

461. In heaven we all respect and understand each other.

462. God does not like robotic slaves to His Will. He seeks those who can help in making his Will and Testament known without lawyers.

463. It is easy to raise your consciousness when you use all the rays.

464. My Lodge is not just a summer retreat.

465. I am an enigma to those who have engineered mistrust and ignored Ma.

466. Download anew the filter of God's

vision into your hard drive each morning.

467. Peace is the reward for those who are relentless in dispensing love.

468. Hurricanes are spirals of man's inhumanity to man and nature unleashed.

469. Reading between the lines requires the secret rays.

470. I can only quicken the elders who have youthful hearts.

September 23, 2005

471. Training chelas is my forte.

472. Eliminate all but the love of the Will of God in your affairs.

473. When I travel I require a fleet fleet.

474. I present to the Lord my best and expect the same.

475. If all life in the universe is one, let's sing our song on pitch.

476. I am a tuning fork, a colander and a blow torch.

477. If Victory is nigh, why not befriend him now?

478. I've known many who began the trek but few who prepared properly to reach the summit.

479. Spirituality arises from humility.

480. As the seasons progress, so do the cycles of the Will of God.

481. Internal combustion is our way.

482. Spirits require light as their food. Soon mankind will also learn this culinary art.

483. Our family planning is solar and galactic evolution.

484. Forfeit your past and fit yourself for a blast of now.

485. Through vicarious at-one-ment with the saints, you will become one.

486. Belief in the power of God must be turned into the real thing.

487. For every divine act I am grateful.

488. My verbiage is similar to Hollywood's: Lights, Camera, Action!

489. Vestments of grace I bestow on those who serve.

490. We are building not only a compelling story but a saga of sages for the ages.

491. Study seashells to discern your origin and your destiny.

492. If you think my eyes are intense, you should see those of my guru's guru.

493. Believe me, my endearing charms have never waned.

494. If truth be known it must first be sown.

495. God is very becoming.

496. Some seek a way in, others a way out. Why not the middle one?

497. The path of the *bodhisattva* is not for flakes.

498. There is a reason why my abode is in the Himalayan heights. Discern it.

499. I am your *coup de foudre*.

500. If all could see the auras of rock stars their music industry would fold overnight.

501. Many seek to touch the hem of heaven but few are willing to become its seamstresses.

502. My turban is composed of light cloth.

503. My goal is to quip you into shape.

September 24, 2005

504. I present a new Morya to you each day.

505. Become palatable to God.

506. Your marathon has consisted of more than one race.

507. Precipitate daily.

508. Embellish your life story in God's Will.

509. Righteousness doesn't have to be self-righteous.

510. Your only quality time is that spent in God.

511. Proper etiquette includes refining your aura.

512. A compelling argument won't work when you aren't.

513. I've learned that there is no final act.

514. Couch potatoes fry themselves.

515. Children love stories, but let them turn the pages.

516. My daily reps include adoration of the Will of God.

517. Know me through correspondence, not just letters.

518. Provide me with proof that God exists *in you*!

519. Vision always precedes Victory.

520. Make your pressing needs more than your dirty laundry.

521. Process from a new paradigm: God's Will.

522. Don't amble, but dash to the finish line.

523. Study Maitreya's Rod.

524. I require caregivers of the Will of God.

525. Be not incessant, but incandescent.

526. Radiate in all directions, including past and future.

527. Victory is volition in compassion to ray forth the *Yod*.

528. Most pianos have 88 keys but more strings. Count them.

529. I am not intense but always at ease in God's Will.

530. I use both telescopic and microscopic lenses depending on the reference I need.

531. Redefine your life daily in God's Will.

532. The stars are populated with cosmic beings.

533. Study the Word.

534. Be picture perfect. Secure the best oils.

535. To know my puns, you must prove that you now see.

536. I am from Sirius, but not always so.

September 25, 2005

537. Study rain.

538. You are a complex equation ready to be solved.

539. Dissolving your karma is better than unraveling it.

540. I am a Cosmic Integer.

541. When you relate to others remember their Source too.

542. Prevent pneumatosis.

543. One's natural inquisitiveness shouldn't lead to another's inquisition.

544. Use only the highest aspects of your memory body.

545. Trains are useful until you begin the final, winding, craggy climb.

546. The Will of God exists everywhere.

547. Learn how much sun you can take each day without being scorched.

548. If you think your tests are difficult, for co-measurement observe ours.

549. Be on the ball while meditating.

550. I am a porthole to the infinite ocean of God's Will.

551. Clipper ships and dinghies have one thing in common.

552. A proposal is best presented on one knee for a reason.

553. We cannot use statues whose makers are stoned.

554. Be nice, but precise.

555. In my retreat we quip elixir by the fireplace.

556. As a child I meditated in trees; now I meditate on them.

557. Light is a profound subject.

558. Don't cohabitate with a mindless being.

559. Present yourself anew to the Great Refiner each day.

560. Total recall is not necessary to hear my call.

561. The study and uses of flowers should be a required course in all prisons.

562. Music unplayed cannot be conveyed.

563. To realize your dream you must first have one.

564. If you are not porous you are not for us.

565. Leap into the arms of the Will of God.

566. If you are not porous you are not for us. Find a new road less traveled.

567. When you are wont to laze, seek my gaze.

568. Magic resides in the predawn hours.

569. I provide cosmic relief.

September 26, 2005

570. Create a new virtue.

571. Study and use waterfalls.

572. Free your mind and then mind your newfound freedom.

573. My life is the Will of God.

574. You should never run out of steam if you remain in my stream.

575. My province is invincible because I provide its fortification—God's Will.

576. To unveil your future tests would create another too great for you to bear.

577. We will have our day. It is today.

578. I learned much from Merlin and you should too.

579. Don't miss the Mark. Call to him.

580. Open a new window of sunlight in your life.

581. The temperamental should remain cool.

582. Even some hellions have halos.

583. Conviviality without spirits is untenable.

584. Empathic knowledge is best.

585. Adepts are not a-dime-a-dozen; they are top-dollar chelas.

586. Provide me a platform and I will speak.

587. Cruelty is the crux of Earth's cross.

588. Project love of God's Will to all.

589. When David saw Bathsheba he should have refrained.

590. Heaven can wait but you cannot.

591. Disassociate yourself with the angry ones.

592. I have a garden too. I prefer asters and forget-me-nots.

593. Study the structure of silicon.

594. Learn to take the heat.

595. I traversed many deserts. That is why I arise early.

596. Purify yourself until you are Pure Self.

597. Lubricate not the engines of war.

598. I prefer the two-edged sword.

599. The Magi still travel together.

600. Neutrinos: your example.

601. Obliterate your own obituaries.

602. Continue our daily communion unabated.

September 27, 2005

603. Contrary to public opinion, I exist.

604. Stay inviolate.

605. God's Will to be known must become your own.

606. Invectives invite disease—to the utterer's dismay.

607. Why repent when you can pant for God's Will each hour?

608. To train your mind you must first lay a straight track.

609. Problems don't arise from nowhere.

610. Creation should be filled with elation.

611. Trust is a must.

612. Confute the enemy into believing you, through kindness.

613. Accept your fate: God = You Now.

614. I employ many servitors of the Will of God.

615. I have many sherpas but carry my own backpack.

616. Prayer must not be an excuse for, but be in support of Being.

617. Pay your debts quickly, then make no more.

618. Hercules and I enjoy a good laugh, but you should hear his!

619. It is easier to make money when you're in harmony.

620. What a great deed: to own the Will of God!

621. Cancel any thought of can't, won't, nought.

622. I believe.

623. In the darkest places I have still uncovered His light.

624. Bring in the new day and a new you.

625. Shine with a new sheen: God's first ray.

626. An image is helpful only when it is becoming.

627. Prepare carefully.

628. Grace results from work.

629. Realize with real eyes.

630. The unconscious is not.

631. Praise creates pure rays to enfold that praised.

632. In enlightened Self-interest praise your Self.

633. Little children have the answers—if you ask.

634. Produce good fruit.

635. Into the blue I go—willingly!

YOUR BUDDHA NATURE
Vehicle for Your Soul's Ascent to Perfect Oneness

Blessed Hearts,

I would speak on your Buddha nature. As you gaze on the image of your Buddha nature beautifully provided to The Hearts Center by the careful brushstrokes of the accomplished artist, Norman Thomas Miller, you see a most glorious rendition in form of the very formless beingness of your divine reality presented in graphic, two-dimensional form. In truth, this Higher Self of you is dimensionless and timeless, co-existing with the very Solar Presence of the One God, the I AM THAT I AM of all life.

As you know, the Buddha is the Awakened One. As the essence of you that is fully awake and all-knowing, this sacred Presence of perfection is the individualized expression of God's light as the monad of who you truly are as a solar being.

The Upper Figure

Tom's rendition depicts the upper figure as a light being circumscribed by seven colored bands of light through which scintillating rays of white light are projected out in all dimensions to bless all life.

This upper figure is your Real Self, the part of you that is fully God and with which your soul, the lower figure in the chart, will merge and fully unite when you ascend into the very heart of God at the close of your earthly incarnations once you truly know who you are, pass all of your initiatic tests, balance the flames of love, wisdom and power within your heart, complete the balancing of at least 51% of your karma and fulfill your divine plan, your life mission.

Your Buddha nature is the allness of God whom you already are but whom you must fully accept and become through letting go of the human ego and lower nature and fully embracing the divine light within. Through surrender of all vestiges of selfhood outside of the circle of oneness of God's being, you enter

Your Buddha Nature
A Chart Of Divine Knowing

into this picture-perfect Presence of ultimate joy, peace and wholeness. You merge with the very heartstream of God that is constantly pouring forth to you all the qualities and quintessences of beingness through the crystal cord that you see in the chart, descending through the middle Buddha figure into your heart chakra.

The Causal Body

Your Buddha nature has access to all the gifts and graces of the Spirit, which you can know in greater and greater spirals of consciousness by tapping into your Causal Body, which is the composite of all of the blessedness of your reality manifest through the good karma, or works that you have accomplished in all past embodiments or lifetimes upon Earth and even on other planetary and solar homes of light. This giant reservoir of perfection is a cornucopia of light-energy as a divine bank account from which you can draw the resources of the Spirit to re-energize your life's mission and fulfill every calling to be an example of grace and holiness to your families, your co-workers, your communities and your entire nation and planet.

The Middle Figure

The middle figure in this chart is the Mediator, or Intercessor, your Holy Christ/ Buddha Self, who knows both the perfection and ideal emanations of your Higher Self while also being aware of the limitations and imperfections of the lower self as it evolves through time and space. This inner teacher is your conscience, which goads you into higher consciousness by reminding you of your inner vows and your true reality. As the abiding presence of inspiration and joy, he leads you to pure beingness as you are silent and listen to that "still, small voice," also known as *the inner man of the heart*.

In this depiction, the Holy Christ/ Buddha Self is seated in the lotus posture, blessing you and all life through a sacred *mudra*, or hand gesture. Behind both the upper figures is the depiction of a rose of light, symbolizing the very nature of elemental love-wisdom that is the essence of God within these aspects of your own being. The upper rose, being more golden, depicts the Buddhic emanation of omniscience, and the lower rose, being more pink or roseate in color and emanation, depicts the love-fires of omnipresence.

The Lower Figure

The lower figure is surrounded by and subsumed into the violet transmuting flame and is also ensconced within the mighty crystal-diamond tube of light, sealing all in a protective action of impenetrable light energy, a sacred forcefield, or flowfield, of divine radiance. This tube of light also surrounds the Holy Christ/Buddha Self, descending from the center of beingness of your Divine or God Presence.

Depictions of the Nature Kingdom

Around the tripartite rendering of your own Buddha nature you see a depiction of nature in its fourfold aspects of earth, water, air and fire with colorful elemental life all about you, providing a platform for your evolving soul in form within time and space. Beloved Tom has spoken of some of the symbology that he painted within this chart, and you may review his commentary to understand the fullness of this tapestry of light that he has graciously provided for all.*

The True You

In truth, you are more than all of this because in your Buddha essence you live, move and have your being in many dimensions of light beyond the physical universe. And yet, this rendering of the True You is a great visual that you may use in your meditations and while giving your prayers, mantras, decrees and songs. For through your sight you tap into the divine world in which your Buddha nature lives and coexists with the One God.

Blessed hearts, utilize this glorious rendition of beingness in your daily life by becoming it fully through all of your spiritual practices. It will only be for you what you make of it through application, through presence, through correspondence. As above, so below, I, El Morya, live within the Buddha nature of the God-reality of all. My presence of joy be with you always.

I thank you.

*Tom's commentary was given during a weekend seminar, Advanced Alchemy, in August 2006, in Minneapolis, Minnesota. It is posted from a link on the *Your Buddha Nature* page at www.theheartscenter.org.

WHO IS GOD?

Who is God? God is the Source, the Creator, the Originator. God is the Undifferentiated, the Unmanifest, the Unnamed, the Essence of all Suchness. As the Sun behind the Sun, God is the Great Emanator. God is complete Beingness. God is Presence. God is The One.

God is the Great I AM. God is Love, Light, Energy, Radiance. All that Is is God. God is Father-Mother, Son-Daughter, Holy Spirit. God is the Great Child, pure and whole. God is the Cosmos, the Universe, the Creation itself, the Ocean. God is the Circle of Life and the Dot in the Center of that Circle.

God is Omnipresence, Omniscience and Omnipotence. God is You. God is Me. God is Us. God is We.

God is the fun way, the simple path, the silly within the Sublime, the sublime within the Divine.

God is the preciousness of each person, the core and the reality of each one's being. God is the revered, and that which is adorable within the reverence expressed, the believable, the lovable and the livable within each one. God is the completeness of all aspects of Selfhood, the jewel in the diamond within the lotus, the full flowering of all qualities and virtues of Life.

God is the Breathing of the Great Inbreath and Outbreath. God is the heart of the matter and what really matters within each heart, as God's own heart-centeredness. God is the sunniness of perfect wisdom, the joy of perfect love, the awesomeness of perfect power. God is playfulness, spontaneity, the laugher of young and old alike. God is the creativity of every artist, the movement of every dancer, the mindfulness of every composer, the mastery of every musician.

God is the expression of every flower, the formlessness of every cloud, the song of every bird, the aliveness of every moment. God is the vibrancy of thoughtfulness and caring, the warmth of a heartfelt embrace, the expectancy of the first kiss, the smile upon an infant when that one is suckling at its mother's breast.

God is the action of lovingkindness, the wisdom behind compassion, the vision of every life mission and the presence behind every form of worship. God is your heart, one with the Divine. God is the First and the Last and all that is between. God is the Alpha and the Omega, the entire alphabet, the Word made flesh and the Word as the *AUM*.

Would you be God this day, I ask? Would you be a new creature, an expression of the Allness of that One? As you express the Word let God be within you.

I am El Morya. This is my message. I Am Real and God is where I Am.

I thank you.

LIGHT ON THE PATH
The Christ Presence within Everyone

Dearest Hearts of Fire,

There is a light that shines for and upon every soul on her pathway home to the heart of God. And this light is the living reality of your Godhood, the grace of beingness in solar joy. I come this day to illuminate your path because you have called to me and my guru, and it is apt and befitting that I do.

The light that lighteth every man and woman and child that cometh into the world is the light of the Christ consciousness.[1] And each one born of God has access to this light, which is the energy and radiance of the Source flowing through the nexus of the Mediator, who is the intercessor for every lifestream, emanating between one's soul and one's God Presence. Through the heart of the Christ, the healing light, which is the transformative power of God to change you from glory unto glory, is manifest for all. This is the miracle energy of the divine, flowing through the Son who also, in his essence, acts as a spiritual sun to shine the radiance of the Father-Mother God to all.

Many look to the Son of God, Jesus, for their spiritual sustenance, for light on their path home to the Creator. And this Son of God so beautifully demonstrates even today how profoundly that light may manifest for the one and for the many who call to him. But few have fully embraced the totality of his teaching and moved into the full stream of his radiance by following the thread of his beingness into the very Sun Presence of who he has become, which they, too, may also become.

It is the living light of the Christ that is the saving grace of Presence that Jesus and all of the saints of God, East and West, would have the disciple of the Spirit know and employ in their lives. It is the essence of beingness as the flow of God's continuous stream of spiritual energy that all must tap into and utilize if they are to fully inherit all that God has in store for his many sons and daughters evolving throughout the worlds and star systems of his creation.

So I come this day to remind you of Jesus' words—that you are all Sons and Daughters of God and that each of you must put on the full mantle of the Christic light, the full garment of grace in order to fulfill your own divine plan and holy mission upon Earth.[2] And it is only when fully understanding the principles and divine laws that Jesus himself mastered and employed in his mission that you can follow his example all the way into the richness of your own reality as a Son or Daughter of God in your own right.

As one who has fully embraced the first ray of the dawn of solar beingness and entered into the very living Presence of God as Jesus has, I speak by direct knowledge from my own witness to that same light that Jesus became, who I also have become. For it was always his desire and motivation that all should follow his example, generation by generation, in the great regeneration of the

Spirit that he so magnificently exemplified in his life of service and sacrifice to humanity.

The light of solar joy may be yours day by day as you enter the very living presence of the Christ in meditation and during holy prayer, as you take time each day to be still and know the I AM light of God within.[3] For the Presence of God is always there for you to know, to love and to grow into, to learn from as you walk the path of light which is the path of the Christ.

Jesus said, "Many sheep have I that are not of this fold"[4] and he was speaking of sons and daughters of God of many other cultures far from his natal land. And today Jesus still speaks and witnesses to that Christic light within all lands and peoples but in a specific way in which they can relate. Do not be surprised if the Christ appears here and there in many other guises but still emanating that glorious light of beingness that shone through him on Easter Sunday and that continues to blaze forth through his divine personage as the Christ to all.

But also be aware that just as Jesus had other sheep, so he has initiated other shepherds of the Spirit to continue his work throughout the world. And these do not always appear and work within the Christian dispensation or the organizations and churches of modern-day Christendom. For should we limit the holy work of the Lord God by our own human understanding? Or should we allow the universality of the Spirit to speak in whatever form it may—through Buddhist and Jain, through Hindu and Muslim, through Jew and Christian, through Native Elders, or even through the heart and voice of a holy child whose heart sings of the divine?

The light of the *Christos* is the light that lighteth everyone who is born into the world. And each one may manifest that light on the path by attuning to the ministrations of the divine within the heart, by accepting the fullness of each day's opportunity to live in the very presence of joy, of love and of grace. You are that light of the Christ as you claim it, as you become it and as you fully radiate it forth into the world, blessed ones.

I am El Morya and I thank you.

1. John 1:9
2. Psalms 82:6, John 10:34
3. Psalms 46:10
4. John 10:16

EL MORYA'S TREASURY OF SPIRITUAL QUIPS

Part Two

September 28, 2005

636. Respect our elders.

637. Travel on the wings of the Will of God.

638. Engender love of the divine gender.

639. Prepare for the worst and expect us.

640. Turn your attitude into gratitude.

641. Invent again what God created.

642. I have a yen for Zen.

643. Gautama has a way about him.

644. Allow me the pleasure.

645. KH and I have also learned to walk on water, but I prefer to run.

646. I study the real stars.

647. My pleasure is always God's.

648. We considered renaming the Great White Brotherhood to be politically correct but Alpha persuaded us otherwise.

649. Value the Will of God.

650. We are causal body builders.

651. Wait on me, never for me.

652. God is the only lovemaker.

653. Be prudent, but never a prude.

654. The Will of God is great.

655. As our children, we remind you to stop, look and listen.

656. The proof is in Buddha's pudding.

657. No jest: The Divine Mother knows best.

658. Our gurus still impress us.

659. Be complete in the joy of God's Will.

660. Maintain your youthful enthusiasm.

661. Collect our thoughts.

662. Master the science of transference.

663. The Keeper of the Scrolls is a real master of the word.

664. Mind my business.

665. Reflect on the Will of God.

666. We grace you with our Presence.

667. I will always be a star-gazer.

668. Are you fully equipped yet?

September 29, 2005

669. Perplexed? Seek God's Will.

670. Surrender means you give upward.

671. Arrangements must be made to allow God back into your life.

672. On the heels of defeat I stand to raise you.

673. I love conviction as long as it is for the light.

674. Joy in the very thought of God's Will.

675. Don't empty your salt shaker as you adore your maker.

676. God knows much more than men give Him credit for.

677. Your real credit rating is above you.

678. Few let me be their personal trainer.

679. Resistance is not only futile, it is useless.

680. Unseat your self-inflicted, wounded self.

681. An infestation of too much ego leads to an unhealthy plot.

682. First-ray masters do not save the best for last.

683. I decided eons ago to serve for life.

684. Some come along for or to enjoy the ride. I prefer drivers.

685. The present and the Presence is all we know.

686. Develop cosmic consciousness. Think outside the galaxy.

687. Cosmic initiations are more exciting.

688. Rally to the real race: The I AM Race.

689. If you're always contesting you're not digesting God's Will.

690. I deliver. What do you expect from a Mercurian?

691. Ascended Masters are more than rocket scientists.

692. In Darjeeling I quickly settle all my scores.

693. I do not believe in waiting rooms.

694. I recommend universal life insurance.

695. Repulsive thoughts lead to spiritual convulsions.

696. Leniency is for the weak-hearted but not for my chelas.

697. Classes in prenatal science and child

development should precede adolescent exploration.

698. God willing, be.

699. My counsel: Confession prevents depression.

700. I require original thinkers.

701. The universe is only one of God's toys.

September 30, 2005

702. Will to be God's Will.

703. Supersize your love.

704. Don't give short shrift to your great uplift!

705. God revels in stellar births.

706. Practical measures always outweigh their imposters.

707. Rest assured that I don't.

708. God's thoughts are precious to behold.

709. Railing against anything will not get you upstairs quicker.

710. Let up.

711. Incorporate your business into the Creator's schedule.

712. The *can do* spirit should be accompanied by the *I AM* spirit.

713. Intelligent design is true evolution.

714. Fast foods lead to a quicker demise.

715. You simply must see the procession of the equinoxes at least once a *manvantara.*

716. Timesharing with the Lord is worth the investment.

717. Our situation room in Darjeeling doesn't lead to one.

718. Position yourself to discern and then to do the Will of God.

719. Shared values must enter the domain of religious ecumenism.

720. Speak softly but carry a big aura.

721. Divine economists ignore petty cashouts.

722. Patent lie number one says: I can't.

723. My appointment book is always open.

724. In heaven, the humblest home is still a palace of light.

725. Hercules has quite a workout schedule!

726. I sing God's Will in all keys.

727. Qigong is a beautiful hand-song.

728. My travels make Gulliver's look Lilliputian.

729. It is wonderful to be a friend of God!

730. Fill your days with works of art and words of the heart.

731. I have entered the miracle mind of my mentor.

732. Dial into your divine frequency.

733. God's angels are his promotional team.

734. Concluding a lifetime of service will win you an eternity of more.

October 1, 2005

735. Flash me a smile. I may reciprocate.

736. Failure to grasp the question leads to self-immolation.

737. Find within each pearl I give you a new beginning.

738. Relate to me.

739. You are a composite of all your past decisions. Posit them in the pool of God's Will and swim with me.

740. My prayer is that you become a perpetual one.

741. Existentialism is the disease of the *Kali Yuga*.

742. Grease the skids of your ascent.

743. Plan accordingly with others.

744. I could write volumes, but prefer

that *you* take up the stylus.

745. Read the stars and then create your own.

746. Buffeted by world events? Consult the captain, for he knows the prevailing winds.

747. Concrete solutions are still temporary.

748. God hopes to include you in his Will and Testament.

749. Your self-mastery can be accelerated by one who knows your map.

750. Gratuities should be earned, not expected.

751. My fortune may be yours if you can believe it.

752. I am happier than you think!

753. Compress time, expand space and watch for me.

754. Photographing the aura will create a new world.

755. Investigative science should always include heartstreaming.

756. Etiquette is synonymous with respect and courtesy.

757. Your comfort zone must accelerate.

758. Age-old traditions shouldn't stifle creativity.

759. Spiritual alchemists must master the compression and attenuation of light.

760. It is simple: truth is self-evident.

761. Presumption of good will does not make it so for all. Insert God's Will.

762. Humility is a stretch for attorneys and physicians, who should be required to walk a day in their clients' and patients' moccasins each week.

763. Value the space in which others exist, but clean up your own first.

764. Pandemic failures occur when hearts have lost the connection to their Source.

765. Meditation on the Will of God must become a prevalent daily practice.

766. Conceptual thinkers should wed boot camp sergeants.

767. I am creating a fertile soil for your springtime rituals.

October 3, 2005

768. The best group therapy is *sangha dharma*.

769. Transportation and teleportation are not so different.

770. Of all the Elohim, Peace carries the largest Sword.

771. Knowledge unused is wisdom defused.

772. God is Joy.

773. Traffic jams of angels answering prayers are acceptable.

774. Fame sought oft comes to naught.

775. Our complex solution is love.

776. When reality sets in, life has meaning.

777. Always be prepared for an honored guest to your hearth and heart.

778. Be free. Watercolor in joy.

779. Vision is both panoramic and focused.

780. Reinvigorate your relationships and labor with a regular back rub.

781. Real growth encourages challenges to ancient paradigms and modern mindsets.

782. Simplify your busy life with love, wisdom and faith.

783. To stay the course you must first have an accurate atlas.

784. There is no discomfort in the heart of God.

785. The Great Initiator knows the exact quotient of fire needed for every soul to pass every test, for he has fulfilled each one in ages past.

786. The universe is a perpetual symphony of divine love.

787. God has a treatise for every soul defining his love and plan for that one.

788. Buddha's life is the supreme model and the sublime example.

789. Be patient. Cosmic planning occurs for every prayer's answer.

790. To rule the roost, first govern your own thoughts and feelings.

791. Graciousness is the byword of every servitor of light.

792. Spiritual relationships will gain you entrée to ports of purity and freedom.

793. Reevaluate your path when you've stayed in a comfort zone too long.

794. Michael desires *Faithful and True* to be approbations for more than himself.

795. Present love is like no other.

796. The road to heaven is lined with right

motive and right action.

797. Perpetual motion is the Mercurian way.

798. Human parenting breeds divine understanding.

799. Visuals and sounds clothe your story with divine feeling.

800. I believe in you now.

October 5, 2005

801. Stake your mark, take your mark, make your mark.

802. Trusting relationships may prove challenging.

803. Compassion requires a divine compass.

804. A valued person gains respect.

805. Increase your fire so no one can put you out or off.

806. Travel in style—ensconced in our love.

807. Joy is the eternal smiling.

808. Leave unfinished business for the heartless.

809. Know my voice in the fire, wind, waves and mountains.

810. Build, knowing that the angels see every step and are helping.

811. Worry not, want for nothing and win.

812. My interjections are for a purpose.

813. Create a fortress within for the divine's residence.

814. Instruct your youth in the science of truth.

815. Replenish your days with service.

816. The mindless ones are not my concern, nor yours.

817. Our abode is sealed from the insane, the profane and the inane.

818. Don't dissect, introspect.

819. Inter second thoughts and enter the first.

820. Invent.

821. Prepare a space where I can converse with you. I prefer the heart.

822. Creation is the birthright of sentient life.

823. Reclaim who you are and have always been.

824. Past tense? Presence flow!

825. Participate in my plan.

826. An air of reverence is the best fragrance.

827. Myrrh is my rhetoric.

828. Sanctify rather than sanction.

829. If you're always responding, you're not on my ray.

830. We work with birds, for they get it.

831. Study and follow the Source's circuit.

832. All study and no work or play is not our way.

833. The Will of God is the first cause and the final word.

October 17, 2005

834. Patience prevents karmic renewal.

835. A valiant heart wins from the start.

836. Protect your investiture of light.

837. Qualify your words with validity, clarity and heat.

838. Realize the necessity of God's Will to act in thee.

839. A profusion of love is the best infusion.

840. I bend time.

841. Space cadets should listen to me more.

842. Conversion is not a matter but a spirit.

843. Replenish your mind in mine.

844. A good laugh renews your cells.

845. Ah, fresh air! Mustiness must go.

846. Prepare for the inevitable—God within, without.

847. Be inclusive—invite every cosmic being to your domain.

848. Dial in to the radio frequency of God's voice.

849. You can handle impending disaster if you choose to.

850. Quality leadership is my responsibility. Sign up now.

851. Your purview must become ours.

852. To know our plan, study cytology.

853. Group think stinks when airheads agree.

854. Violence is not our way; inviolate action is.

855. Trap your thoughtless words and express only the sublime.

856. Cosmic input; cosmic outflow.

857. Those who evaluate others should keep their work to themselves.

858. Conduct a reality check daily.

859. A quality life is God's desire for all.

860. Expand space through the Will of Grace.

861. Vie not, die not. Be and see.

862. We are always in training. That's the fun of it.

863. I play in peonies, pansies and petunias.

864. Forge your union with the ion of the One.

865. Propel your mind into the domain of cosmic knowing.

866. There is more to come for those who come to More.

October 24, 2005

867. I make the impossible doable.

868. What I imply you must ply.

869. Trust in the process of loving the Will of God.

870. Important work always awaits the faithful chela.

871. Profound insights inspire the diligent seer.

872. Quality faith must be pursued.

873. I am only intense to those who slack me.

874. Divine reality hovers.

875. A purposeful life is your birthright.

876. Reveal to others only that which you've become.

877. Giddy students best *giddyup*!

878. Prevalent among mankind are those who don't prevail enough.

879. Unzip the true you now.

880. Deafening is the drumbeat of the dissident. Outpace them.

881. Been there, done that? Really? Then come and find me!

882. Progressive teachers must remain ardent students.

883. If you tend to regress, egress without regret.

884. Finding the talisman requires a keen sense of smell.

885. Your cells already have the full indoctrination of their Sun-Source.

886. Put your past behind you and your last ditch attempt beneath you.

887. Increase the flow of cosmic plentitude throughout.

888. Vibrate within the divine accelerator of God's Love.

889. When reality sets in, seek a new and higher one.

890. If you're not having fun, get more sun!

891. Goalfitting is an exciting art.

892. Making your ascension is a daily reality.

893. Pretend, contend, intend and lastly tend.

894. I seek present voices, not echoes.

895. Godly men and godly women must become fully God.

896. Enjoy your daily walk with God, for He does.

897. Come and posit your positive thoughts in mine.

898. Value life and yours will increase.

899. If you only fend for yourself, you'll never find your Self.

900. Training continues unabated for the pros.

901. I love prose pros.

October 25, 2005

902. The proof is in the plodding.

903. God's Will is my expertise.

904. Get involved in cosmic evolution.

905. An embrace of grace is worth my pace.

906. Pretentious ones never get it.

907. Don't guffaw when you violate the law.

908. If you offend the Lord, don't expect a ready ear.

909. Firm masts outlast prevailing winds.

910. Being true requires more than being blue.

911. Vanquish the sense that you lack.

912. Play the game of divine life.

913. Drama queens must be unveiled and false kings unmasked.

914. Jumpstart your day with a shot of God's Will.

915. All need my God-speed.

916. Hearsay—bah! Hear me say, RA!

917. Will you help me stoke the fire?

918. Flim-flam chelas never catch the flame.

919. Obtuse blockheads have infiltrated your universities. It's time for new minds.

920. Don't bolt before you molt.

921. Caring for a newborn foal should be a prerequisite for all doctoral candidates.

922. Intrepid financiers are needed.

923. Quality dictations are here.

924. Predate yourself.

925. Compile the best light resumé.

926. Intelligence is a dividend of wisdom.

927. Confine your patience to all except yourself.

928. Unhitch your ties from those who pull on you.

929. Contest your acceptance of mediocre spirituality.

930. Pure thoughts ought to be the world norm.

931. Valiant reliance on perfection releases creative sparks.

932. Your job is to extend potentiality into fulfillment.

933. Crude prudes don't exude our style.

934. Rally around the flame of cosmic truth.

935. Treason begins with small ideations of rebellion.

936. Seeming tragedies have impelled many to godhood.

October 29, 2005

937. Face it: you're all biracial.

938. Complete surrender is easy when your head is on the block.

939. Purity of motive is the best votive.

940. Prepare for your full victory and then accept it manifest now.

941. Partial plans never work.

942. Tomorrow's dreams cannot be fulfilled—only today's.

943. Lessen your load; become a porter.

944. Depending on your point of view is fruitless.

945. Give all and then live well.

946. Stop begging. Accept your needs met now.

947. Repeat after me: I AM all that I AM.

948. Quality means the quiet acceptance of light in you now.

949. Graciousness multiplies mercy.

950. Always dismiss thoughts, feelings and words of lack, unknowing and fear.

951. Those who generate fear are not our advocates.

952. Obsess and compel only in God.

953. A broad smile goes a mile abroad.

954. Don't endear others to you; clear yourself to serve others.

955. Victory now! Wow, wow, wow!

956. Woo others only to the Real You.

957. I light candles in the wind. Can you?

958. Presumptuous ones don't know my ray.

959. All that awaits you has always been.

960. Don't ask us to cover for you; discover yourself.

961. Study eye movement, structure and color.

962. Intuit motives, needs and means.

963. We resist those who insist.

964. Cosmic travel is easy when you have no baggage.

965. If you condone error you'll never fly.

966. Spiritual flight is governed by light.

967. Greater works are being done.

968. Don't wallow in the past, swallow it.

969. Reinvent yourself hourly.

970. I talk with you more than you care to realize.

971. Friendship with God is your natural estate.

972. All need God's Will and Testament.

973. Arrest thought of aught but what God hath wrought.

974. I need quality reps.

975. My relationships are all meaningful.

976. Portend the Divine You now.

977. Violate every human limitation.

978. Respect your divine beginnings.

979. Don't become a nuisance to your Self by allowing others' attempts to change you.

980. Taking the next step shouldn't require prolonged meditation.

981. Let my voice be your sonic boom.

982. I suggest becoming co-dependent with KH and me.

983. Those who put on airs have not respect.

984. The pool of my love awaits your daily dip.

985. Yes, KH and I have raced up the tall pines of Darjeeling. Guess who won?

986. Light untrammeled must through you be channeled.

987. The densest derelicts still maintain within the divine seed.

988. Wear my jacket, my children.

October 30, 2005

989. Processes that edify are what we investigate.

990. Program your life to be fluid, radiant and potent.

991. Arriving at your goal doesn't necessitate a long stay.

992. An ounce of compassion is worth a pound of apology.

993. Vibrant souls generate great lift.

994. Your divine worth was seeded at birth.

995. Venerate only the living and giving ones.

996. My chelas never tire of leaving fresh tracks on the mountain of attainment.

997. Problem solving is the game of life. Our smile is your best assist.

998. Inducing resonance among you all is my joy.

999. Only teachers who have carved new pathways are worthy of your time.

1000. Precipitate a new dimension of love in all you do.

Art," God echoes it back to you.

1022. The relentless pursuit of the divine does have its payday.

1023. In his heyday God designed you and me.

1024. Quality visuals are hard for you to find, though we have a vast collection.

1025. Macrobiology is underfunded.

1026. The past one should learn most from is one's own.

1027. A good interpreter must speak between the lines.

1028. Kind hearts attract.

1029. Contentious as it may be, I recommend uninhibited passion for God's Will.

1030. My troops know my voice but also my step.

1031. Inveigle yourself in God's doings.

1032. Humans are strange: They accept unbridled public displays of affection with elemental life but not among those of their own kind.

1033. In God we trust one another.

1034. The gift of Pure Will I bestow when you least expect.

1035. Make a grand entrance to the stage of life even if you haven't mastered your lines.

1036. A brisk walk with me will avail you much.

1037. If you think microbiology is an exacting science, try examining the lives of our chelas!

1038. Bleeding hearts don't make effective probation officers.

1039. Corporate bigwigs should be sheared regularly.

1040. Snooty politicos don't frequent my retreat.

1041. I have been known to confide in the Elohim.

1042. Practicing the Presence makes you perfect.

1043. I avoid fellowship with mindless politicians like the plague.

1044. Chip away daily at your unfinished business.

1045. Practical applications should be the only kind.

1046. Seeing what a mustard seed produces, I was inspired to cultivate myself.

1047. True leaders have become an endangered species.

1048. Most political correctness is best abandoned.

1049. Just beyond the horizon I exist.

1050. I entrust few with my plans and so should you.

1051. Awareness: define it, then refine it.

1052. Home is where the heart sings.

1053. Meditate on effulgence.

1054. Cosmic potential is available to all.

1055. True bliss is never monotonous.

1056. I was a Sikh but now I am found!

November 4, 2005

1057. Your quality time should be every moment.

1058. Prevail even against all prevailing winds and ideas.

1059. Fortuitous events await those who do the Will of God.

1060. Binding agreements oft require loose-leaf paper.

1061. Preparing for every possible outcome is pernicious. Prepare for God's.

1062. Sikhs should find a kind word always.

1063. Pleasant dreams are muses' gifts to the pure in heart.

1064. Unbridled violence is never condoned but a sure and able defense a requisite.

1065. Resuscitate your childhood vivacity daily.

1066. Collaborative works create a wider audience.

1067. Understanding your Self will elicit greater compassion for others.

1068. Contemplate the Divine Mother and you shall enter her fruitful womb.

1069. Realization shouldn't require being argumentative or insipid.

1070. Valiant thoughts create idyllic matrices through which angels easily enter.

1071. Contend against the selfish needs of nihilism.

1072. Profound meditations require purity, practice and patience.

1073. The Divine never dotes on pretentious chelas.

1074. Gracious practices create a blest, new world.

1075. Invite every angel to be a witness and an *aide-de-camp* to your work.

1076. Guile must be routed from your mannerisms, mien and mind.

1077. Even our best servants need a breather from our rays.

1078. Intention sets the sea for a smooth sail.

1079. Travel with your best jacket and your brightest smile.

1080. Introduce me to those whose lives are full of light work.

1081. Imperative is our involvement in the affairs of mankind.

1082. Incursions into the dens of darkness are not for the weak-spirited.

1083. The probability of your success increases as you focus on God's Will.

1084. Intuition should be the basis for all rational thought.

1085. True creatives are those who do not merely mimic, but who rise to see and penetrate beyond the veil of mortal actions.

1086. By tying yourself to God you loose the bonds of human inertia.

1087. Palpable answers to life's daily dilemmas are my specialty.

1088. Increase wisdom by accepting solar radiance within your mind and heart.

1089. Struggle not to transcend this plane but to accept your divine estate already bequeathed during your first breath.

1090. Animal magnetism must be overcome by your selection of nature's gift of purity.

1091. Star clusters are celestial group hugs.

1092. Wise is he who invests in his own

spiritual development, for the return will aid many other limpid portfolios.

1093. Creative solutions must become your daily fare and avocation.

1094. To penetrate my mind you must first be kind.

1095. Your relatives are your best opportunities for self-mastery and surrender.

1096. Your primal imperative must be God's Will.

1097. Guardians who lack compassion often reincarnate as the unwanted.

1098. Eject every vestige of self-pity, doubt and guile.

November 19, 2005

1099. Spiritual training requires an enlightened coach. Try me.

1100. A graduated plan that fosters acclamation of and acclimation toward the ascension is our way.

1101. Godly men and women must become the common example for the youth.

1102. Divine inspiration requires an air of expectancy and a miracle mindset.

1103. Volatile situations are best defused first through a hearty laugh and then expert, conscious speech.

1104. Triumphant are those whose wills are steeled, whose minds are sealed and whose hearts are healed.

1105. Incorrigible delinquents often have the stuff of future heroes. Fully love and value them through their temporary depravity.

1106. Accumulate wisdom through deep meditation on holy verse.

1107. Spiritual portals are meant for us to leap, not gaze through.

1108. Spiritual training requires an enlightened coach. Try me.

1109. Profound are pros who have found God's Will.

1110. The Holy Spirit must be invited daily for he is an itinerant.

1111. Reluctant students make lackluster teachers.

1112. If you're not graduating from something daily your mortar is stale.

1113. Behemoth appetites are best left at the door.

1114. Sun cities are my vision of the future.

1115. Proud parents should first speak of others' children's virtues.

1116. Let our WMDs be blue/yellow lightning and laser fiats on mass entities.

1117. Repeat offenders need relief through purple/emerald memory showers.

1118. When you are composed, the Great Composer may direct you.

1119. Your delusions of grandeur must give way to real visions of splendor.

1120. Practice first the art of self-mastery

and all others will come easily.

1121. Great expectations create a field of belief that will make them so.

1122. Unknow who you aren't.

1123. Meditating on the Cosmic Void creates new wormholes to Infinity.

1124. Illumination is a matter of increasing your wattage to match God's socket.

1125. Study the science of refrigeration to learn to cool your jets.

1126. Flu is easily consumed by the astute fire bearer.

1127. Erase the blueprint of your not-self.

1128. A God-directed life is the only one of value.

1129. Know the midpoint between relative good and evil.

1130. Opportunity knocks but only you can open the door.

1131. Relegate your past to the dung heap of mediocrity. Stand and BE now!

1132. I am arming you with the fervor, the gnosis and the attitude of Victory!

December 12, 2005

1133. Eradicate the space between you and God.

1134. Profess only truth with each breath.

1135. Find in God's Will the key to each day's enigmas.

1136. Vegetarians are the best veterinarians.

1137. Pour your heart into your work, words and world.

1138. Contending with evil will only prolong the battle mode.

1139. Renew your bodies with energetic breathing, visuals and music.

1140. Valuing others' time will help dissolve its grip on you.

1141. Finding the answer doesn't mean you've applied it yet.

1142. If pride goeth before the fall, then don't trip twice.

1143. Gain altitude through a positive attitude.

1144. Meeting a true heartfriend is meeting God in the flesh.

1145. Glow!

1146. Refresh your spirit with a new outlook and release on life and love.

1147. Porcupines were created to elicit tender loving care.

1148. The dynamics of becoming God must be the new science.

1149. Failure to apprehend the bad guys and the truth leads to the same rut.

1150. Compress your analysis into cosmic vision of the oneness of all and then the details will become self-evident.

1151. Always proving yourself right leads to the left-handed path.

1152. Your best finery should be reserved for your spiritual garments.

1153. Sewing up one's tattered auric rents is the first exercise at Luxor.

1154. Complaining eventually leads to deplaning from God's transport.

1155. Spiritual virtuosity is the daily expression of all ascended beings.

1156. Once perfected, let every creation be released; then begin a new and more refined one, learning from your last effort.

1157. Wordsmithing is not so difficult when you have become the Word.

1158. Prove not why but how others may benefit from your daily striving.

1159. Study liquid infusions, and then accelerate them into etheric renderings.

1160. One day you will opt for the internal computer of God's reasoning.

1161. Joy in the experience of relearning God's reason for you to be alive each day.

1162. Finding another's niche should not require abandoning your own objective view.

1163. Fantasies gain a foothold only as they are energized by your light and attention.

1164. Adepts still perform spiritual calisthenics to remain toned and attuned to the One.

1165. Grace has thousands of expressions but always issues from the same divine givingness which is pure love.

1166. Replete with wisdom, you must use it or lose it.

1167. Failing to yield to the Divine One will manifest in a poor yield.

1168. Find your niche and then continue your hide and seek with God.

December 13, 2005

1169. True friends are reminders and advocates of who you are.

1170. Hercules provides me with cosmic relief.

1171. Granted, I am your true friend.

1172. Dispensations are gainfully secured and painfully lost.

1173. Freedom to flaunt the law should not be used as an opportunity to do so.

1174. Intervening in your affairs is often a delicate and unrewarding proposition.

1175. Contravening the Will of God is a nasty pre-position.

1176. Your aura speaks volumes even when you don't.

1177. Infuse and conclude each work with a

lasting impression—God's.

1178. Knowing the ropes requires none around your neck.

1179. Provide me with clay and I'll fashion a winner.

1180. Jesus saw what was required and made it happen—my kind of guy.

1181. Interference is every demon's preference and attempt to inter you with mediocrity's temporal laurels.

1182. I am often terse with verse.

1183. Unkind words bind you hand, foot and mouth.

1184. Be introspective to gain God's perspective.

1185. Discover the true meaning of love through my heart.

1186. I uncover the real thing—You.

1187. If you're truly in tune with me, then I won't stop your song.

1188. Violate always the law, lay and lie of mortality.

1189. If you'd increase your speed make sure you're heading true north.

1190. Attempts to control others always lead you backwards.

1191. Gains are easily lost through a lack of self-control.

1192. I chide and ride only those who hide from themselves.

1193. Don't be conflicted; be confident in the confluence of God's Will.

1194. I'd rather be fishing for those who want the whole enchilada—God.

1195. Intense struggles are for those who haven't fully surrendered.

1196. That which you revisit regularly you shall become.

1197. Singing is one way the angels breathe.

1198. Great things await those who glorify God in all they do.

1199. Refining one's own jewel is a lifetime work.

1200. The haughty are half-wits.

1201. Reflect upon God's voice, which ever echoes throughout the cosmic egg.

1202. We, too, know high finance and have set our plans in motion.

1203. My flower arrangements consist of my blessed chelas' variegated works.

1204. Let your only intention be to please God.

WHAT IS A SPIRITUAL DISPENSATION?

A dispensation is a grant of energy that ascended masters secure on behalf of Earth's evolutions in order to provide opportunity for spiritual growth through a specific movement, project, teaching or endeavor. The dispensation is approved by various cosmic councils based on the nature of the request and usually requires a promise of repayment in the form of the spiritual growth, greater enlightenment, practical work and prayer support of or from those to whom the dispensation is directed.

At times the grant is only made when spiritual collateral is offered by one or more masters until the debt of light is repaid in full. The process is not unlike the securing of a loan from a bank or a grant from a charitable fund, organization or sponsoring philanthropist.

The Hearts Center movement is a dispensation of grace secured by various sponsoring ascended masters who sought to have another voice or amanuensis through which the Universal Great White Brotherhood could communicate their love-wisdom teaching to mankind. The original sponsoring masters of The Hearts Center are The Great Divine Director, Mother Mary, El Morya, Lanello and Kuthumi. On January 1, 2008 Lord Lanto replaced Kuthumi as a sponsoring master.

WHAT IS A DARSHAN?

The Bridging between the Divine and the Human

by El Morya

A darshan is a time of intimate communion between a master and that one's disciples where spiritual radiance and blessing is released both in the teaching and instruction conveyed and also in the very presence of the master. A field of awareness as a radiance of light energy is created by the master that is expanded through the chakras and aura of the master through the messenger around the disciples as divine wisdom, timeless truths and universal principles are expressed through discourse and conversation.

Within The Hearts Center movement, a darshan is an opportunity for disciples to ask questions of the master and receive a direct reply. At times a darshan has also been a session when the master asks questions of disciples to elicit or educe their own inner wisdom gleaned through their spiritual path, their training and evolving consciousness.

A darshan is a holy experience of oneness with God. It is a timeless journey into the unknown by placing one's self at the feet of the master to receive progressive revelation in the Now. It is a time of contemplation upon the deeper mysteries of life where the master often releases a new wisdom teaching never before revealed in the context of the present reality of life of the individual disciple or student of light.

Within The Hearts Center, time has been set aside during the devotional family services on the first Sunday of the month for a live darshan for youth and adults alike. Darshans occur regularly during the regular six to ten-week Meru University classes held by teleconference or via the internet throughout the year. Darshans often occur during the major quarterly conferences and local weekend seminars as well as the extended international pilgrimages sponsored by The Hearts Center.

The intimate communion heart to heart

through the heartstreaming of the love-wisdom fires of the master with the disciple is the miraculous manifestation of the conveyance of solar radiation for the enlightenment of every student. The master seeks to convey something of his own essence, of his own experience of the path of beingness as an immortal one to those still evolving in time and space. This bridging between the divine and the human and the human and the divine is the creation of a portal between the heaven world and the earth itself.

Through the voice of the messenger, the bridge is oiled and the open door is sustained. Through the mind conveyance, as a telepathic communication, virtue flows and radiance grows as each devotee is able to sustain the tie to the master through acceptance, belief, devotion and the residing within of peace. The discourse is the vehicle for the increase of light within the world of form and the soul and beingness of the student.

All teaching is a means to the end of the enlightenment of the disciple, his ultimate freedom. When embraced and assimilated, the light within the instruction, as a seed of fire, grows within the ascending one as a divine sprout that that one may follow through all the coursings of the soul into the divine world. It is as if you are Jack rising upon the bean stock as it first penetrates the earth and then grows into the outer limits of Earth's atmosphere penetrating the plane of the human into the divine.

Each darshan experience is a holy conveyance of spiritual fire as an impetus of light that the disciple may utilize for his victory, for the fulfillment of the mission, for the balancing of the scales of karma and for the garnering within the greater community of a unity field of awareness between all disciples.

The master takes the opportunity of receiving one question to enlighten all at their level of understanding. And so there is conveyed in the answer, molecules of light that can grow within each one at that one's level of attainment, of divine gnosis. This the master does with great alacrity, with great God-mastery because he or she is attuned to the level of the vibration of the Real Self, the Solar Presence of each disciple. And in holy communion with that one's higher reality he extends the grace directly from the Higher Self through the vehicle of the teaching to inculcate greater God-beingness within all.

As each disciple is sensitive to the ministrations delivered through the chakras of the master through the messenger and lovingly and reverently receives the instruction and at times the discipline of the light through the message, all are raised as the soul of the one is raised. Thus there is the enfiring of the *antahkarana* of the entire hierarchy through any master's discourse and teaching. Elemental life, angels, unseen masters, devas and divine spirits witness this alchemy of the transfer of light and beingness and also receive the currents of love-wisdom through the heart of the master through the mind of his solar radiation.

It is as if during each darshan and

discourse, the sun comes to the earth through the solar beingness of the master and enfires all within the radiance of that solar light with the golden liquid Christ-essence, Buddhic beingness of the master. This is a type of cosmic photosynthesis whereby the photonic energies from the Solar Source of the master is conveyed and is synthesized within the divine factory of beingness of the soul of the disciple as that one is able to assimilate and sustain the light and the photonic particles within the teaching.

The divine science of every darshan is magnificent to behold and should be understood in the context of the higher science of the Spirit whereby the kingdom of heaven comes to earth through the greater blessing of beingness of the one sent, the master unto his disciples.

Glory-by-glory and one-by-one the Earth is raised through the sacred *sangha*—a community of hearts that resonates as one crystal, one great focus of the Lord God and the Universal Great White Brotherhood. Respect, courtesy, reverence and humble acknowledgement of the master's presence serve the disciple to receive the fullness of that which he would convey. It is a grace. It is a miracle manifestation of light that all should appreciate, revere and glory in the awesomeness of the One.

Thank you, blessed hearts, for your attention, the focus of your love, your deep devotion to holy purpose and the New Blue light of Alpha and Omega come to Earth.

I thank you.

WHAT IS THE ASCENSION?

The ascension is the natural and final initiation for souls who are ready to merge with their Source or Divine Presence. During this sacred ritual which is beautiful to behold, the soul is divested of every last vestige of darkness and limitation and is subsumed completely into the glorious brilliance of the Solar light of pure beingness in God. This individualized flowfield of energy is also known as the personal I AM THAT I AM or I AM God Presence.

Souls go through a process of both involution and evolution in their sacred journey through life, and the ascension is the final act in this grand saga and drama. Having learned the lessons of life, the ascending one has balanced at least 51% of her negative karma, brought into balance the divine spark of life known as the threefold flame within the secret chamber of the heart and fulfilled her divine plan or life mission in service to humanity. By mastering the initiations of the seven rainbow rays the soul attains Christ Consciousness by focusing the light of God through the pure crystal or prism of Selfhood.

There are 33 major initiations on the path to wholeness in God and the ascension is the final or 33rd step in the rising, spiral staircase upon which the soul evolves. Having mastered time and space by awakening from duality to embrace the unity of being through heart centeredness, the soul passes its tests and graduates from Earth's schoolroom. It then begins a new life as an immortal being, never more to partake of the human condition with its limited concepts, but living fully within the liquid, crystal light energy of God's Spirit of oneness, having access to the Universal Mind, living in the nirvanic realms of light, joy and freedom.

I AM THE ONE!

1. Come, O diamond Will of God,
within my aura blaze.
Now radiate protection here,
all life on Terra raise.
God-power streaming from above,
your strength of purpose win
Determination in your ray,
perfection grow within.

Refrain: I Am the One, I Am the One,
I stand in Morya's fire;
I Am the One, I Am the One,
I live in God-desire!

2. Come, O diamond Will of God,
defend my very soul.
Blue lightning, flash across the sky,
O heal and make me whole.
Unite all people in your ray,
forget-me-nots now bloom.
Unshackle every child of God,
unworthiness consume.

3. Come, O diamond Will of God,
the dweller now reprove.
Intensify the sacred fire
and guide my every move.
O strip me of all lesser loves
through Morya's steely eyes,
Let *virya* and integrity,
belief and faith arise.

ABOUT THE HEARTS CENTER COMMUNITY

The Hearts Center is a new opportunity for spiritual seekers to receive up-to-date inspiration from the ascended masters whose caring and love are tangible in their worded releases. The Hearts Center is not so much an outer organization as it is a movement of hearts that are united in love-wisdom to pursue their own individual calling and mission with divine abandon, full of expectancy and with a heart attuned to divine ideals and holy purpose.

The Hearts Center believes that the ascended masters, those who have mastered time and space and now serve as our friends, mentors and guides, such as Jesus, Kuan Yin, Saint Germain, Mother Mary and Gautama Buddha came to Earth to demonstrate that what they could do we also can do, as the fullness of divine potential lives within the heart of each one of us.

The Hearts Center Community lives by the Golden Rule. We respect the right of each individual to decide the rate of his or her own spiritual progress on the path.

Guided by ongoing revelation from the ascended masters, as given to their messenger, the Community works together in harmony and compassionate wisdom, with each one offering their unique gifts and talents for the benefit of all sentient life. We believe that spiritual practices such as prayer, mantra, music, meditation and visualization can focus and concentrate the Light of God for personal and planetary transformation.

Meru University, the adult educational component of The Hearts Center, is a modern-day mystery school that facilitates the spiritual development of the soul. The university is dedicated to the sharing of ageless wisdom and progressive revelation through courses, seminars, workshops, publications and projects. These courses assist seekers in understanding the ancient and modern teachings of East and West.

Each year, the ascended masters propose the messenger and the Hearts Center Community go on a pilgrimage to sacred sites in different parts of the world. The mission of the pilgrims on these sacred journeys is to anchor and emanate spiritual light to heal the heart of the planet and her peoples.

The Hearts Center Community believes that the family is sacred, and that the family is the basic platform for the evolution of the soul. Meru Learning Centers are being established to educate children in cosmic principles that enhance their connection with their inner spiritual teacher, for the realization of their divine potential.

The Hearts Center Community is in the process of establishing a home with a spiritual sanctuary and business offices in the heart of Paradise Valley within the beautiful Rocky Mountains of south-central Montana.

You may view our introductory video free on-line as well as read the transcripts, listen to the audio files or see the videos of other instruction by El Morya and many other ascended masters. For more information, we invite you to visit our website at www.theheartscenter.org. You may e-mail us at friends@theheartscenter.org, or call us at 630-894-4410.

Thank you for completing this leg of your spiritual journey with us!

OUR DECLARATION OF SPIRITUAL FREEDOM

We, the lightbearers of The Hearts Center, joyfully unite to continue the spiritual work of the ages through daily and ongoing revelation from the Ascended Masters as given to their anointed Messengers. Reaching out to serve all life, we dedicate our hearts to world freedom and to bringing forth the plans of beloved Saint Germain and Portia for the Golden Age of Aquarius—a time of peace, harmony, joy and beauty.

Hearts Centers are vibrant communities of joyous companionship and love. Filled with the presence of the Holy Spirit, these centers around the globe are places where the sacred fire is invoked to transform our lives and our planet.

We welcome all seekers of truth, honoring their talents and religious backgrounds as we offer spiritual practices, educational programs and community fellowship to enhance their growth in the study of the deeper mystical teachings of the world's major religions. Our hand of heartfelt friendship is extended to one and all.

We live by the Golden Rule and respect the right of each individual to decide his rate of spiritual progress. We champion the freedom of each individual to make independent, informed political and social choices. Learning to live with one another in harmony, with compassionate wisdom and surrender to the Will of God, we humbly offer any gifts or training that we possess for the benefit of all. We speak and serve with kindness and charity. Regardless of age, culture, station in life or financial standing, we uphold the divinity within one another so that a golden age may swiftly come.

We are committed to a renaissance of beauty and culture that transforms lives, moving Earth closer to the original divine blueprint by making the gold mine of Ascended Master teachings readily available through all media and technology as well as conferences, pilgrimages, healing seminars and heartstreaming sessions held the world around.

We support golden age concepts of economics and energy utilization. To this end, we encourage such practices as yoga, tai chi, qigong, foot zonology, holistic medicine and the mindful eating of healthy foods. We understand the importance of cooperating with the ecology of this planet, for our physical and spiritual health are one with it.

We further believe that the harmony we embody occurs through attunement with our individualized Divine Presence as we maintain a state of listening grace. In collaboration with heavenly masters, angels, and nature spirits, we are assisted in achieving ever-increasing intimate communion with God. We practice spiritual sciences such as meditation, prayer, mantras, visualization, songs and rituals to heighten our attunement and to bless all of life. And we experience sacred darshan with the Ascended Masters.

Understanding the importance of the Holy Family as the basic platform for the soul's evolution, The Hearts Center sponsors Meru Learning Centers.

These learning centers are dedicated to educating the souls of children in cosmic principles that enhance the connection with their inner teacher. Our Aquarian Age model of education provides an environment for parents to work side-by-side with their children using a free choice, hands-on curriculum composed of spiritual lessons, meditations and various practical and creative applications of cosmic law.

These experiences set a standard of excellence in education and culture that develops the inner potential of the soul of each child in their zone of proximal development. A repository of curricula and parenting guidelines is available to all parents and teachers. Interactive workshops are conducted around the world.

Meru University is a modern-day mystery school that assists in the spiritual development of the soul. The university is dedicated to the dissemination of ageless wisdom and progressive revelation through courses, seminars, workshops, publications and projects. The university assists all seekers in understanding the ancient and modern teachings of East and West brought to life by commentary from the Ascended Masters. Our programs are an open door for learners to walk and talk with the Ascended Masters daily, preparing our students to become spiritual leaders, teachers and ambassadors of divine love-wisdom to the world.

The Hearts Center promotes the mission of Saint Germain, avatar of the Age of Aquarius, and his teachings on sacred alchemy for the uplifting of ourselves and our planet. Through the Violet Joy Solution, his energetic gift of spiritual transmutation, we witness the power of forgiveness, mercy and freedom. By study and day-to-day application of the violet fire, we aspire to self-transformation, which, in turn, transforms the world.

At Hearts Centers, heaven touches earth

and hearts connect the world around. Our beloved Masters engage with us in holy exchanges of love-wisdom fires, and our cup overflows with gratitude as we live in the reality of this cosmic interchange. Our greatest joy and deepest desire is to share this elixir with all who seek spiritual freedom.

Yes, love-wisdom is the elixir of The Hearts Center!

ABOUT DAVID CHRISTOPHER LEWIS

David Christopher Lewis is a mystic, spiritual teacher, composer and author for the Aquarian age.

Raised Catholic, David embraced the concepts of karma and reincarnation when he was just 14 after reading Edgar Cayce's *The Sleeping Prophet*. For the next three decades, David studied the world's major religious traditions, albeit through a more mystical, esoteric lens. For twenty-two of those years he lived and worked in an intentional spiritual community.

He married in 1986, and has three children. In 1994, he opened and managed a highly successful art gallery and framing business, which he sold in 2005.

In the spring of 2004, David had a mystical awakening and began receiving regular telepathic communications from enlightened spiritual beings known as ascended masters. He maintains that he is not *the messenger* for the ascended masters, but rather *a messenger*, affirming that all of us can and should develop our own spiritual faculties as well.

Early in 2005, with seven others, David founded a spiritual group known as The Hearts Center. This non-profit organization, dedicated to helping people everywhere connect with and nurture their own divine potential, has grown in the last three years into a world-wide movement with local centers in two dozen cities in the United States, Canada, Latin America and Europe.

The Hearts Center maintains a website: www.theheartscenter.org, where over eleven hundred HeartStreams, or inspired discourses from the ascended masters that David has received, are published in audio, print, and recently, in video format as well. David coined the term *heartstreaming*, and co-authored with Michael McNeil a chapter on this subject for the anthology, *Healing the Heart of the World*, published in 2007, by Elite Books.

David regularly conducts prayer and meditation services and teaches during free internet broadcasts on The Hearts Center's website. He has also written and published extensively over the last three years. Among his published works are a collection of more than 150 devotional prayers, songs and mantras, guided meditations, and instruction on the spiritual science behind sungazing.

Since 2005, David has traveled extensively to sixteen countries while leading pilgrimages to Mexico, South America, Egypt, Europe and the Far East and conducting nearly forty seminars and conferences in the United States, Canada and Europe.

NOTES

NOTES

NOTES

NOTES

NOTES